O-PEDIA

VOLUME TWO
MORE STINK-Y STUFF FROM A TO Z

Megan McDonald   illustrated by Peter H. Reynolds

CANDLEWICK PRESS

A Ask Stink

Ask Stink

Get all the dirt on your favorite character . . .
right here.

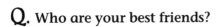

Q. What's your real name?

A. James Edison Moody.

Q. Who are your best friends?

A. Webster, Sophie of the Elves, and Skunk.

Q. What's your favorite book?

A. The *S* encyclopedia.

Q. What's your favorite food?

A. Silver-dollar pancakes.

Q. What would you say is your proudest
moment?

A. Rescuing 101 guinea pigs.

Ask Stink

Q. What's your favorite candy bar?

A. It's a three-way tie between PayDay, 100 Grand, and Milky Way.

Q. Who is your favorite president?

A. James Madison.

Q. Do you have any pets?

A. Mouse, my cat; Toady, my toad; Astro, my guinea pig; and I used to have a newt named Newton before Judy flushed him down the drain.

Q. What pet do you wish you had?

A. A stick insect or a blue-tailed skink.

Q. What's your best super-galactic idea?

A. Saving Pluto.

Ask Stink

Q. Are you a member of any clubs?

A. I am a member of the Toad Pee Club.

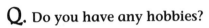

Q. Do you have any hobbies?

A. Drawing comics and bugging my sister.

Q. What do you hope to be when you grow up?

A. A professional smeller.

Astronomical Animals

Stink likes to think that when class 2D's pet newt slipped down the drain (oops!), it went on to great adventures. And what greater adventure is there than a trip into outer space?

The United States, the Soviet Union, France, Japan, and China have all sent animals to outer space. Some of the lucky (?) animalnauts:

★ The very first creatures ever sent into space were fruit flies.

★ On June 14, 1949, Albert II, a Rhesus monkey in a U.S.-launched V2, became the first monkey in space.

★ The first animal sent into orbit was the dog Laika, launched aboard the Soviet *Sputnik 2* spacecraft on November 3, 1957. The longest space flight by a dog is twenty-two days.

★ The first fish in space was a mummichog.

Astronomical Animals

★ Ten newts with cut-off limbs were aboard *Bion 7* in 1985. Scientists studied the limbs as they grew back to understand how humans might recover from injury in space. Ouch!

★ Arabella and Anita are the first spiders to go to space. They got to eat filet mignon!

★ Japanese tree frogs visited the Mir space station in December 1990.

★ Mice, guinea pigs, stick-insect eggs, Mexican jumping beans, crickets, and Madagascar hissing cockroaches have all been sent into space, too.

B Big and Little

Good things come in small packages. Just ask Stink! And big things come in, er, big packages.

★ The world's smallest mammal is the bumblebee bat.

★ Will the real World's Largest Spider please stand up? *Megarachne servinei*, the World's Largest Spider, is a fake. It's more like a crab or sea scorpion. That's **GOOD** news for the Goliath birdeater, the **TRUE** world's largest spider.

★ Some hummingbirds weigh less than a penny.

6

Big and Little

★ The blue whale's head is so wide that a team of 50 football players could stand on its tongue.

★ The baby blue whale drinks up to 100 gallons of milk per day.

★ The longest earthworm ever measured was 21 feet long, found in South Africa.

★ The longest species of snake is the reticulated python, which can grow to a length of more than 30 feet.

GROSS!

DID YOU KNOW?

If your tongue could do what the nectar bat's tongue does, you'd be able to lick your own toes while standing up.

Brainy Cat

You may not be able to tell just by looking at her, but the Moody family cat, Mouse, might just be a genius.

IS YOUR CAT A GENIUS?

Can your cat read a map?

    Yes   No

Does your cat meow at the fridge when hungry?

    Yes   No

Does your cat take cat naps?

    Yes   No

Does your cat have a good memory?

    Yes   No

Does your cat wake you up like an alarm clock?

    Yes   No

Can your cat get you to let it outside?

    Yes   No

Can your cat express emotions?

    Yes   No

Brainy Cat

How many times did you answer YES?

1–3 Send your cat back to kitty kindergarten

4–6 Super Cat

7 Phi Beta Catta — Genius!

> Takes after me, I guess!

Turn to page 134 for more brainy cat facts!

C Carnivorous Plants

Jaws, the Venus flytrap that belongs to Stink's sister, Judy, has a taste for flies and raw hamburger. Pass the ketchup, please.

◎ The snap "trap" on the Venus flytrap takes less than a tenth of a second to SNAP.

◎ If a Venus flytrap doesn't like its prey, it will spit it out within 12 hours and start over.

HEY, BIG MOUTH!

Other names for Venus flytraps:

Jaws   Fused Tooth

Sawtooth

Red Piranha

DID YOU KNOW?

It was once thought that the first Venus flytraps caught a piggyback ride on meteors, crash-landing here from outer-space.

Carnivorous Plants

OTHER TRICKY TRAPS USED BY CARNIVOROUS PLANTS:

- **Pitfall:** prey falls into a pool of dew or nectar collected inside of a rolled leaf.

- **Flypaper:** prey gets stuck on sticky, mucus-like glue.

- **Bladder:** prey gets sucked into the vaccum-like trap.

- **Lobster pot:** easy to enter, but no way out!

Cars

Stink sleeps in a bed shaped like a car, but in his dreams he drives these for-real wacky wheels:

Cars

★ The jet-powered Flatmobile is the world's flattest vehicle, reaching only 19 inches from the ground.

★ Who needs a house when you own the longest custom-built car in the world? With 24 wheels and measuring 100 feet long, the Cadillac limo has room inside for parties beneath its crystal chandelier. Head to the roof for a soak in the hot tub or a dip in the swimming pool.

★ What do Newton and Toady and the Surface Orbiter have in common? They can all travel on land and in the water. Rick Dobbertin of New York spent four years turning a shiny silver milk tanker into a funky amphibious ride.

DID YOU KNOW?

The U.S. has 200 million cars. That's 40% of the world's total, and the most of any country in the world.

D Dirty, Stinky, Yucky Jobs

Stink wants to be a professional smeller when he grows up. Here are some other jobs that really stink!

Bat Pee Club!

Guano may sound like a fruit, but it's bat poop! And your job, should you choose to become a bat cave scavenger, is to collect bat poop. You will need a raincoat, boots, and a willingness to get peed on all day.

Golf Ball Diver

At 9 cents a ball, you can make six figures a year by diving in lakes for golf balls and recycling them for reuse. You will need a tetanus shot, the ability to see in the dark, and a healthy fear of water moccasins and alligators.

Roadkill Cleaner

Three hundred thousand big-game animals are killed on U.S. highways every year. Somebody has to clean 'em up. Enter: Roadkill Cleaner.

Dirty, Stinky, Yucky Jobs

Owl Vomit Collector

Your job, should you choose to be an avian vomitologist, is to collect owl pellets for use in science classes. Night owls needed!

Sticky Business

Rod Fudge is a leech trapper. He catches as many as 15 tons of leeches (by hand!) a year, which he sells to bait shops.

Disasters

Stink has had his share of disasters—orange hair, falling asleep on the school bus and missing his stop—but nothing like these real-life catastrophes!

◎ In the Chandka Forest in India, elephants went crazy during a severe drought and heat wave. On July 10, 1972, a stampede of elephants charged through five villages, killing 24 people.

Disasters

◎ In the Great Boston Molasses Flood, on
January 15, 1919, a huge cast-iron tank
containing molasses burst open. Two million
gallons of molasses poured down the street,
killing 21 people and injuring 150.

◎ As the rigid airship the *Hindenberg*
prepared to land in Lakehurst, New Jersey
on May 6, 1937, a small fire erupted near
its tail fin. The ship's highly flammable
hydrogen fuel was ignited, and the
Hindenberg exploded and burned up, all
within 34 seconds. Amazingly, more than
half of the 97 passengers survived.

◎ In AD 79, the volcano Mount Vesuvius
erupted in Pompeii, Italy, and lasted for
two days. When it was over, the entire
city was buried under 30 feet of
lava, mud, rubble, and ash.

Earwax E

Judy: Hey, Stink, what's that sticking out of your ear?

Stink: None of your earwax!

CERUMEN is the fancy scientific name for earwax.

Speaking of earwax, got too much of it? Try chewing gum or talking; that'll help massage your ear canals and loosen up the wax.

WHAT IS EARWAX FOR?

It blocks dust and other stuff (Hello, bugs!) from getting into your ear.

In medieval times, painters used some way-weird stuff to make colors: carbon, chalk, rock, gold, silver, and . . . earwax!

Earwax has a bitter taste. You know what that means, don't you? Somebody actually ate the stuff!

DID YOU KNOW?

The first lip balm was actually earwax! Eee-yew!

F Fingerprinting

No two fingerprints are exactly alike, so if Judy has been touching Stink's stuff, he'll know (as long as she doesn't wear mittens)!

- Even identical twins do not have the same fingerprints.

- Dactylography is NOT the name of a newly discovered dinosaur. It's the study of fingerprints.

- Taking the fingerprints of criminals goes back to the time of King Hammurabi (1792–1750 BC).

- The FBI has a database called IAFIS (Integrated Automated Fingerprint Identification System) that holds the fingerprints of over 51 million bad guys (and girls)!

- A koala's fingerprint is almost identical to a human's!

DID YOU KNOW?

Like fingerprints, everyone's tongue print is unique, too.

Fingerprinting

Humans have three main types of fingerprints: arch, loop, and whorl.

ARCH

LOOP

WHORL

Freaks of Nature

Stink thinks Judy
might be a freak
of nature. She's
what you get when
you cross a human
girl with a bug:
a great big pest! Check
out these for-real nature bloopers.

ꙨNEWSꙨ

MEET ME IN ST. LOUIS
A rare, two-headed albino rat snake
named We lived in the World Aquarium
at the City Museum in St. Louis until 2006.

AMAZON PINK RIVER DOLPHINS
While most dolphins are gray, these have
blood closer to the surface, giving the skin
a pink appearance.

Freaks of Nature

SHARK FOOT!
Mary Looi of Malaysia was getting ready to prepare and cook a shark for her family when she discovered that the baby shark had webbed feet!

OWL HEAD
Martin Laurello was able to swivel his head 180 degrees like an owl, making it look like his head was sometimes on backward.

SIX FINGER DISCOUNT
When Antonio Alfonseca pitched for the Philadelphia Phillies, his nickname was The Octopus, or Six-Fingers. He has six fingers on each hand and six toes per foot.

G Glow in the Dark

Stink loves his glow-in-the-dark pajamas. They're comfy *and* scientific! Check out these other bright spots!

- Mosquito Bay in Puerto Rico contains 700,000 tiny organisms per gallon that flash a blue-green light for one-tenth of a second, making it the largest glow-in-the-dark bay.

- Fireflies use flashes of green light to attract mates. Each species has its own special flash pattern.

- **Fooled ya!** The cookiecutter shark glows a pale blue-green that looks just like the ocean. Only one small dark patch on its belly doesn't glow. That spot fools other fish into thinking that it's a tuna. Then, SNAP!

Glow in the Dark

⊚ A certain kind of squid can squirt out a cloud of glow-in-the-dark "ink." Hidden by the glow, it makes its escape.

OTHER THINGS IN THE NATURAL WORLD THAT CAN GLOW IN THE DARK:

- Butterflies
- Mushrooms
- Jellyfish
- Potatoes
- Octopuses
- Centipedes

DID YOU KNOW?

Using a satellite, scientists have discovered a huge glow-in-the-dark "milky sea" the size of Connecticut floating in the Indian Ocean. What's making it glow? Bacteria!

Great Wall of China

Stink and his friends build their own Great Wall of China out of empty cereal boxes. But the real wall would never fit in Webster's backyard!

It is thought that the real Great Wall of China, constructed around 210 BC, is made of an estimated 3,873,000,000 individual bricks or blocks, and took more than 2,000 years to build.

The Great Wall is not really one long wall, but many walls that snake along a 4,000-mile path, long enough to stretch from New York City to Houston, Texas, and large enough to be seen from outer space.

DID YOU KNOW?

In its life span, an ant colony can move as much.as forty thousand pounds of soil. That's the ant equivalent of the Great Wall of China.

Great Wall of China

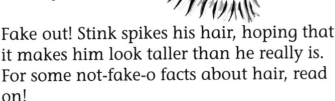

H Hairy Facts

Fake out! Stink spikes his hair, hoping that it makes him look taller than he really is. For some not-fake-o facts about hair, read on!

★ The human head has over 100,000 hairs.

★ At any given time, 90% of the hairs on your scalp are growing while the other 10% are resting.

★ Hot weather makes your hair grow faster.

★ The life span of a human hair is 3 to 7 years. That means some of Stink's hair might still be baby hair!

★ A head of hair is so strong it could support the weight of two elephants.

★ A scientist can figure out where you live and what you had for breakfast by studying just one hair on your head.

DID YOU KNOW?

The first tennis balls were stuffed with human hair.

Hairy Facts

HAIRY . . .
Anthony Victor of India has a 7-inch-long ear hair!

HAIRIER . . .
The longest beard ever measured (17 feet 6 inches long) belonged to Hans Langseth of Norway. The beard was donated to the Smithsonian Museum in 1967. Hans Langseth was not.

EVEN HAIRIER . . .
Xie Qiuping of China holds the record for World's Longest Hair: 18 feet, 5.54 inches. She's been letting it grow since 1973.

HAIRIEST!
The Gomez family of Mexico holds the world record for being the hairiest humans on Earth, with 98% of their bodies covered in hair.

DID YOU KNOW?

Ancient Romans dyed their hair with bird poo.

Homework Excuses

Hey Stink! Where's your homework?

My sister, Judy, used it for her Christmas list.

What happened to YOUR homework?

- My Venus flytrap ate it.
- It got sucked into a black hole.
- Mom recycled it.
- Dad was trying out his new paper shredder.
- Kitty litter . . . need I say more?
- I decided to save a tree instead.
- My house is a Homework-Free Zone.
- I learned to JUST SAY NO.
- It was arrested by the Homework Police.
- I left it on top of the Empire State Building.
- You just can't see it because it's written in invisible ink.

I Insects

Stink's favorite insect is—what else? The stinkbug!

Don't squash that bug!
The stinkbug lets go a vile odor through holes in its abdomen to keep from being eaten by birds and lizards.

Would you eat a stinkbug?
In South Africa they do. Stinkbugs are a good source of protein, fat, amino acids, minerals, and vitamins.

DID YOU KNOW?

In insects, the brain has four parts.

THE BUZZ ON MOSQUITOES

If you were a mosquito, would you rather bite:

a. a kid

b. a grown-up

a. a brown-haired person

b. a blond person

a. someone wearing a pink shirt

b. someone wearing a black shirt

a. someone who just ate a banana

b. someone who just ate meat loaf

a. someone who is asleep

b. someone who just ran a marathon

Turn to page 134 for the answers!

DID YOU KNOW?

Megan McDonald wrote a book about eating bugs. For research, she ate a toasted mealworm and a roasted cricket!

Invisible Ink

Stink enjoys mixing up potions, like Anti-Sister Repellent and *Eau de Toilette*. Here's a recipe he might try when he's in a top-secret mood.

Better not try this with your math homework, or you might get an invisible grade!

1. Squeeze the juice of one lemon into a small cup or bowl.

2. Use the juice as ink by dipping a cotton swab or paintbrush into the lemon juice.

3. Write your message on paper.

4. Let it dry.

5. Hold the paper up to sunlight or a light bulb (heat source).

6. Voilà! Your secret message will turn light brown, so you can read it.

Now try "painting" over the paper with purple juice. Your secret message should appear in a color!

Invisible Ink

OTHER THINGS THAT CAN BE USED AS INVISIBLE INK:

- Cola drinks
- Milk
- Vinegar

- Honey
- Onion juice
- Pee (P.U.!)

Can you read the message below?

Turn to page 134 for the answer!

Jack Frost **J**

Jack Frost is the name of the Moody family's new mail carrier. Jack Frost (aka Old Man Winter) is also the name of a mythical, magical person who paints frosty designs on windows, leaves, and grass when the temperatures drop below freezing.

Here's how folks from other parts of the world refer to that coolest of the cool:

- Jokul Frosti (Scandinavia)

- Grandfather Frost (Russia)

- Old Mother Frost (Germany)

- Frostman and Mistman (Japan)

- Pleiades, or the Seven Sisters (Australian Aborigine)

DID YOU KNOW?

No way! Way! One of Megan McDonald's sisters lives in Minnesota and has a mailman named Jack Frost.

Jinx

Same-same! Jinx is a game to play when two people accidentally say the same word or words at the exact same time. There are many ways to play the game.

- Be the first to yell, "Jinx, you owe me a Coke" and (lightly!) punch the other person in the arm. They owe you a Coke!

- Be the first to yell, "Jinx!" Start counting fast: "1, 2, 3, 4, 5 . . ." until the other person yells, "Hot chocolate!" The last number spoken is the number of hot chocolates you're owed. (Candy bars work, too!)

- If you're the first to yell, "Jinx," the other person can't speak until someone calls them by name.

- In California jinx, the person jinxed can't go to the bathroom until someone calls them by name!

Jinx

◎ In Chicago, the jinxee has to take off his pants and hang around in his undies until somebody calls him by name!

◎ In New Zealand, the first person to finish saying, "Jinx, jinx, jinx, personal jinx, caps lock, lock up, smash key, throw away crumbs" is the jinxer. Try saying that three times fast!

K Ka-Ching!

More on Stink's favorite subject—MONEY! He likes getting it, collecting it, counting it, studying it . . . spending it! Wonder if he knows that James Madison once appeared on a 5,000-dollar bill! For real!

MONEY, UP CLOSE AND PERSONAL

DID YOU KNOW?

China was the first country to use paper money.

★ Can you find an owl hiding on the front of an American one-dollar bill? Look in the upper right-hand corner, to the left of the number 1 in the shield. Some say it's a spider!

★ On the reverse side of a hundred-dollar bill (aka a C-note), the hands of the clock in the steeple of Independence Hall are set at approximately 4:10.

★ Count 'em! A dime has 118 ridges around the edge.

Ka-Ching!

FUN WITH MONEY

★ Ask a friend if he can find *1776* on a one-dollar bill. (It's at the bottom of the pyramid, and appears in Roman numerals: MDCCLXXVI.)

★ Ask a friend, "How many times does ten appear on a ten-dollar bill?" Give him a minute to study the ten-dollar bill. He will probably guess 11. (Actually, it appears 12 times, because *ten* can be found in the words *legal tender*.)

DID YOU KNOW?

If you toss a penny 10,000 times, it will not be head 5,000 t but lik T

Knuckleheads

(Aka gotchas and groaners.) Stink is one smart cookie. Think these tricky questions would trip him up? Try them for yourself, or try them on a friend. Who's a knucklehead?

1. What color is the White House?

2. What president was Washington, D.C., named after?

3. *Antidisestablishmentarianism* is a very long word. Can you spell it without looking?

4. If Mrs. Birdwistle's peacock lays an egg in her neighbor's yard, who owns the egg?

5. What is the eleven-letter word that most spelling bee contestants spell incorrectly?

6. Does England have a fourth of July?

7. What was the president's name in 1976?

8. How many animals of each kind did Moses put on the ark?

9. What are cornflakes made of?

10. Where do the biggest potatoes grow?

11. When is an ant not an ant?

12. drop a yellow hat in the Red Sea, what become?

13. popular cheese is made backward?

Turn to page 135 for the answers!

times,
more
4950.
e heads
picture
weighs
more, so it
ends up on
the bottom
more often.

41

Leap Year L

Q: When is your birthday the day after today but not tomorrow, and the day before tomorrow but not today?

A: When you're born on February 29/Leap Day but it's a non-leap year.

★ Stink is a "leapling." That means he was born on February 29, which only shows up on the calendar once every four years. That makes Stink technically only one year old!

★ February 29, or Leap Day, is added to the calendar every four years because the earth does not orbit around the sun in exactly 365 days. The Egyptians were the first to come up with the idea of adding one day to the year every four years to keep the calendar in sync with the solar year.

DID YOU KNOW?

Olympic Games and U.S. Presidential elections are held every leap year.

43

Leap Year

★ Your chances of being born on Leap Day are about one in 1,461. Altogether there are about 187,000 people in the U.S. and 4 million people in the world who were born on Leap Day.

★ The Henriksen family of Norway holds the record for the most kids in one family born on Leap Day. All three children were born on February 29!

DID YOU KNOW?

In Greece, getting married in a leap year is bad luck.

Lighthouses

When Stink and his family visit Ocracoke Island, he gets to see a very old lighthouse. Every lighthouse sends out a unique series of flashes. Some even blink out a message in Morse code.

The tallest lighthouse in the U.S.:
Cape Hatteras lighthouse, 208 feet

The tallest lighthouse in the world:
Yokohama Marine Tower, Japan, 324 feet

◎ One of the Seven Wonders of the Ancient World is The Lighthouse of Alexandria, in Egypt. It took 20 years to build and was as tall as a 45-story skyscraper.

Know what message the Ocracoke Island lighthouse flashes? One way to find out is to read *Judy Moody & Stink: The Mad, Mad, Mad, Mad Treasure Hunt!*

DID YOU KNOW?

Lightships were used where the water was too deep to build a lighthouse. Lightships hung lights at the tops of their masts. In foggy areas, the ships sounded a bell, whistle, siren, or horn.

Lighthouses

⊚ The Point Lookout Lighthouse in Maryland is said to be haunted. Doors open and shut for no reason. Ghosts talk. One ghost, dressed in a long blue skirt, is thought to be Ann Davis, former lighthouse keeper!

⊚ Minot's Ledge lighthouse near Boston, Massachusetts, flashes 1—4—3, blinking out the message "I love you."

LOL (Laugh Out Loud)

Stink is always yucking it up. All that laughing is good for his health and his super-size brain. No kidding!

Health experts have found that laughing makes a person feel better and actually helps fight disease. It can reduce stress and protect the heart, help the brain stay alert, and take away constipation.

Wanted: Laughers

Madan Kataria of India started the Laughter Club. Anybody who likes to laugh may join! To date, there are more than 3,000 laughter clubs in the world.

World Laughter Day

is celebrated all over the world on the first Sunday in May. LOL!

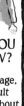

DID YOU KNOW?

On average, an adult laughs about 15 times a day; a child laughs 400 times.

(The *M* is silent!) Stink uses a mnemonic to remember the names of the planets:

My Very Educated Mother Just Served Us Nine Pizzas

(**M**ercury, **V**enus, **E**arth, **M**ars, **J**upiter, **S**aturn, **U**ranus, **N**eptune, **P**luto)

It feels like cheating, sure, but it's not!

Here are more tricky tricks to help you remember important facts:

COLORS OF THE RAINBOW:

ROY G. BIV
(Red, Orange, Yellow, Green, Blue, Indigo, Violet)

THE GREAT LAKES:

HOMES
(Huron, Ontario, Michigan, Erie, and Superior)

MVEMCJSUNPE

Mnemonics

THE ORDER OF THE SIX STRINGS ON A GUITAR:

Eat All Dead Gophers Before Easter
(E A D G B E)

LINES OF A MUSIC STAFF FROM BOTTOM TO TOP:

Every Good Boy Does Fine
(E G B D F)

THE ROMAN NUMERALS FOR 50, 100, 500, AND 1,000:

Lucy Can't Drink Milk
(L=50, C=100, D=500, M=1,000)

SEVEN CONTINENTS:

Eat An Aspirin After Any Nighttime Snack
(Europe, Asia, Africa, Antarctica, Australia,
North America, South America)

Monstets

Being a bit of a shrimp, Stink is obsessed with all things monstrously gigantic, even the ones that may or may not be real!

BIGFOOT AND NESSIE

Many monsters, such as Bigfoot or the Loch Ness Monster, have never been proven to exist. But they have never been proven to not exist, either!

★ Bigfoot, also known as Sasquatch or Yeti, has been described as being six to ten feet tall and weighing more than 500 pounds. The first "evidence" of Bigfoot was a photograph of a footprint taken in 1951. Since then, Bigfoot sightings have been reported all over North America.

★ Luckily for Sasquatch, in Skamania County, Washington, there is a law that prohibits the killing of Bigfoot!

> Think you've seen a Sasquatch?
> Go to **bfro.net** (website of the Bigfoot Field Researchers Organization) and report it!

DID YOU KNOW?

A major Bigfoot sighting took place in Stink's home state of Virginia in 1995.

Monsters

ANYONE UP FOR A SWIM?
The Loch Ness Monster, also known as
Nessie, is a creature said to inhabit Loch
Ness (**LOCH** means **LAKE**) in Scotland.
Although no physical evidence of Nessie
has ever been discovered, some say that
she might be related to an extinct
species of reptile, the Plesiosaur.

Do your own Nessie research! Go to
http://www.nessie.co.uk/view.html
and view a video of the lake. Look for
strange shapes or ripples in the water!

Monsters

Nessie may be the most famous lake monster, but many other lake monsters have been sighted in other parts of North America:

Ogopogo (British Columbia, Canada)

Cressie (Newfoundland, Canada)

Maggot (Newfoundland, Canada)

Mishipashoo (Ontario, Canada)

Illie (Alaska)

Tahoe Tessie
(Nevada and California)

Tarpie (Florida)

Slimy Slim (Idaho)

Eelpoot (Maryland)

Mishy (Michigan)

Pepie (Minnesota)

Oogle-Boogle (Montana)

Mosqueto (New York)

N Nerds of the World, Unite!

Stink reads the encyclopedia for fun. From time to time, he imagines that he is a superhero. He finds math relaxing. Some might say he's a nerd-in-the-making. He says it's cool to be smart. How about you?

SCORE ONE POINT FOR EACH "YES" ANSWER.

1. Is your ceiling covered with glow-in-the-dark constellations?

2. Do you carry a pen that will still write in outer space?

3. Does your lunch box have a lock with a secret code to open it?

4. Have you read all seven Harry Potter books and attended at least one midnight book party?

5. Do you take tests just for fun? (This one counts!)

6. Do you plan to apply to college by the time you are in third grade?

7. Do you celebrate Pi Day? Mole Day? Square Root Day?

8. Do you boldly go where no man has gone before?

9. Do you collect comic books?

10. Have you invented your own time machine?

Nerds of the World, Unite!

HOW'D YOU SCORE?

1–3: Sorry — uncool. Go read more comic books and try again.

4–6: Need more nerd. Go watch more sci-fi movies and try again.

7–9: You are definitely in the nerd zone. You pass.

10: All hail Captain Nerd!

DID YOU KNOW?

Spain celebrates Nerd Pride Day on May 25. There, a nerd is called a *friki.* Freaky, man!

Nerds of the World, Unite!

Once you pass the Nerd Test, you are ready to take the Nerd Oath:

1. I will spread the nerd word: it's stinkin' cool to be smart.

2. I will never leave home without a comic book.

3. I know what a tesseract is.

4. I am always ready and able to name seven superheroes at a moment's notice.

5. I will create at least one invention before my ninth birthday.

Newts and Other ^{state} Amphibians

You've probably heard of state flags, state flowers, and state birds. But state amphibians? It's true! Class 2D's red-spotted newt proudly represents the state of Newt Hampshire. Other facts about state amphibs:

★ Most state amphibians are frogs.

★ New Mexico claims the only toad.

★ New Hampshire is the only state to have a newt.

★ The bullfrog has some stiff competition for State Amphibian of North Carolina. It's up against the Pine Barrens Tree Frog (way cute), the Snot Otter (way cranky), and the Neuse River Waterdog (huh?).

DID YOU KNOW?

Rhode Island, the smallest state, has the shortest state motto: Hope.

57

Newts and Other ^state Amphibians

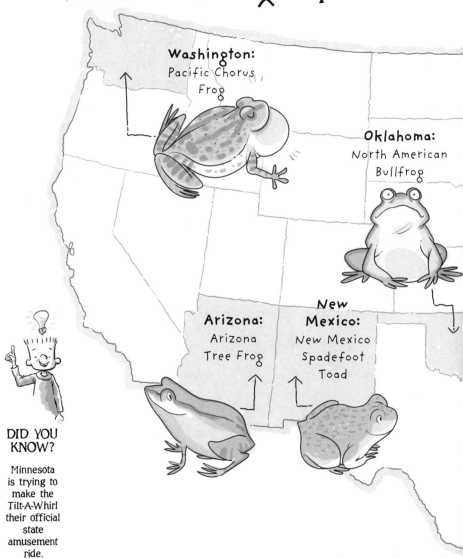

Washington: Pacific Chorus Frog

Oklahoma: North American Bullfrog

Arizona: Arizona Tree Frog

New Mexico: New Mexico Spadefoot Toad

58

Newts and Other State Amphibians

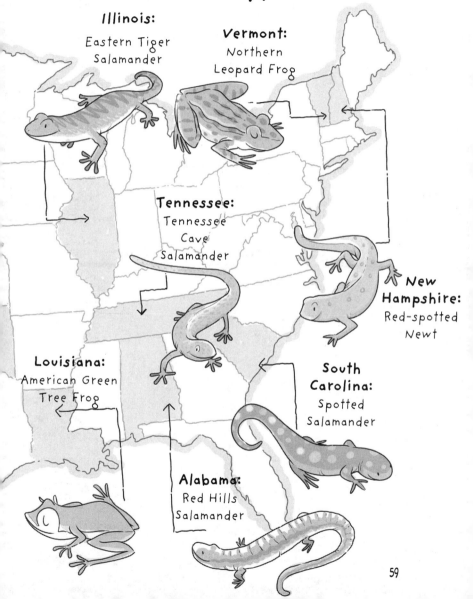

Illinois:
Eastern Tiger Salamander

Vermont:
Northern Leopard Frog

Tennessee:
Tennessee Cave Salamander

New Hampshire:
Red-spotted Newt

Louisiana:
American Green Tree Frog

South Carolina:
Spotted Salamander

Alabama:
Red Hills Salamander

Night Owls

'Tis the night before Christmas, and Stink is trying to stay awake to see snow on Christmas Eve! Too bad he's not nocturnal.

SOME REAL NIGHT OWLS

- ◎ An owl's eyes can spot a mouse a football field away on a moonless night.

- ◎ Bats get around in the dark by a kind of sonar called echolocation.

- ◎ Small lemurs are nocturnal. Even their name comes from the Latin *lemures,* meaning "nocturnal spirits."

- ◎ Earwigs are nocturnal. They may have gotten their name because people believed the insect would crawl into their ears at night.

- ◎ Pit vipers use heat-detection to catch prey at night.

Crepuscular is not a kind of muscle! It means that an animal is active at dawn and dusk.

Creepy Crepuscular Critters:
red panda, cat, dog, deer, firefly, moose, rabbit, chinchilla, ferret, guinea pig, hamster, common mouse, skunk, rat, and capybara.

DID YOU KNOW?

Many birds migrate at nighttime, using the stars and constellations to help guide them.

O Origami

Be a member of the Toad Pee Club! Make your own origami toad.

> You'll need:
>
> ◎ a 3 x 5 index card
>
> ◎ pencil(s) or marker(s)
>
> ◎ lemon juice (Hardee-har-har!)

1. Place index card on a flat surface as shown.

2. Bring corner A to edge B, crease, and unfold. Bring corner B to edge A, crease, and unfold. You should now have a big X-shaped crease on the card.

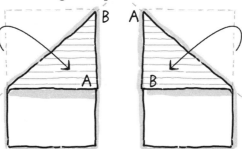

Origami

3. Turn the card over. Draw some toady eyes and nostrils if you like.

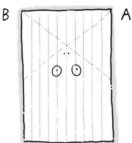

4. Fold the X-shaped crease in half, crease, and unfold.

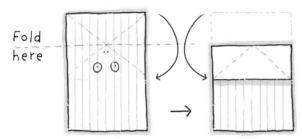

5. Turn the card back over. Gently poke the middle of the X-shaped crease to create a scoop in the card.

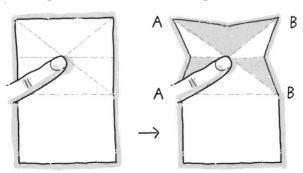

Origami

6. Bring point A to A and B to B. Flatten the triangle shape this creates by smoothing it with your hand.

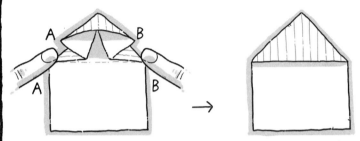

7. Bring corner B to point C and press to flatten. Bring corner A to point C and press to flatten. These are your toad's front legs!

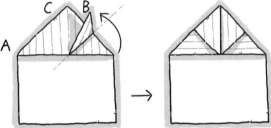

8. Bring the two long sides of the card in so that they meet in the middle. Press to flatten.

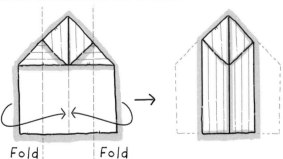

Fold   Fold

Origami

9. Bring bottom edge A to C and gently crease.

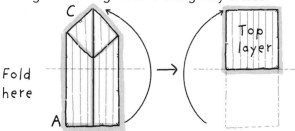

10. Fold top layer in half by bringing top edge to bottom edge. Turn it over to see your handiwork.

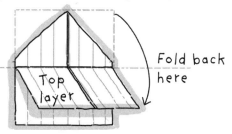

11. To make your toad hop, flick the edge of its back lightly. The stiffer the paper, the higher your toad will hop!

Go to **www.stinkmoody.com**
to print out your very own
Toad Pee Club membership certificate!

Outer Space Jokes

To a Pluto and Saturn freak like Stink, space is no joke. Except when the joke is all about space, that is.

DID YOU KNOW?

The line above Earth where outer space begins is called the Kármán Line.

What planet has the best s'mores?
Mars has all the Mars-mallows.

What galaxy do cows love most?
The Milky Way

What's the best dessert to eat in space?
Moon pies.

What do they call the Fourth of July in outer space?
The Big Bang.

What did Jupiter play on his iPod?
Nep-tunes.

Outer Space Jokes

Where do all the Dalmatians in outer space live?
On the Dog Star.

What do you call a long walk in space?
A star trek.

Why did Mr. and Mrs. Dipper get a divorce?
They were having star wars.

Why did the astronaut's pants fall down?
He forgot his Kuiper belt.

What do squirrels eat in outer space?
Astro-nuts.

Why won't Pluto take a bath?
He'd rather take a meteor shower!

DID YOU KNOW?

It's impossible to snore in outer space because of weightlessness.

Pizza P

October is National Pizza Month, but Stink will eat pizza any month of the year, any day of the week! In fact, he eats 23 pounds— or 46 slices—of pizza per year. That's how much the average person in the United States eats in one year.

Americans eat about 100 acres of pizza per day! That's 350 slices of pizza being eaten every single second.

And kids ages 3—11 choose pizza over mac and cheese, burgers, chicken nuggets, and hot dogs as their favorite meal.

DID YOU KNOW?

The most popular pizza topping is pepperoni.

Pizza

MOVE OVER, ANCHOVIES.
HERE ARE SOME REALLY WEIRD
PIZZA TOPPINGS:

marshmallow and chocolate (a s'more pizza)

fried eggs

hamburgers, fries, and ketchup

grapes and pickles

DID YOU KNOW?

Most pizza delivery orders are called in by people while they're watching the weather report on TV.

Pizza

★ Save your pennies! Nino's Bellissima in New York City sells a pizza that costs $1000! That's $125 a slice. It's topped with lobster and 6 kinds of caviar (fish eggs!).

★ And the prize for all-time world's weirdest pizza topping goes to: stinkbug pizza!

★ But wait! In Japan, there is a special pizza that's topped with squid ink instead of sauce!

DID YOU KNOW?

Peter Reynolds once ate a chili hot dog pizza. Three classics in one!

Pop Poop Quiz

Everybody poops—Mouse, Newton, Astro, even Stink, the little stinker. And you! Yes, you! But how much about that common thing, poop, do you know?

1. Ancient Romans dyed their hair with:

   a. cow dung
   b. pigeon poop
   c. dog droppings

2. Your poop is mainly made of:

   a. chewed-up pizza
   b. leftovers
   c. water

3. By the time you are 70 years old, you will have pooped a pile as big as:

   a. a car
   b. a bathtub
   c. the Empire State Building

4. Why do dogs eat poop?

   a. It smells mmm-mmm good.
   b. They have to eat twice to get all their vitamins.
   c. They mistake it for a dead mouse.

Pop Poop Quiz

5. During the Civil War, bat poop was used to make:

   a. gunpowder
   b. soup thickener
   c. bandages

6. Which animal's poop smells as sweet as candy?

   a. guinea pig
   b. cat
   c. pony

7. How did the first astronauts poop in space?

   a. They dumped it into outer space.
   b. They held it for the length of the space mission.
   c. They froze it into poop-sicles.

8. Which one of these is a nickname for poop?

   a. black banana
   b. lincoln log
   c. floaties

9. What famous person said, "Never kick a fresh turd on a hot day"?

   a. President Harry S. Truman
   b. Bart Simpson
   c. Shakespeare

Congratulations! You now have a load more info on poop.
Turn to page 135 for the answers!

Q Quicksand

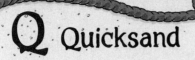

Better watch your step, Stink!

Help! I'm sinking! Quicksand is sand or grainy soil that shifts in a semi-liquid state. The word *quicksand* means "living sand."

IF YOU FALL INTO QUICKSAND, WHAT SHOULD YOU DO?

1. Scream at the top of your lungs.

2. Get your sister to pull you out by the hair.

3. Send your dog to get help.

4. Wish you had done your homework about quicksand.

5. Be glad you have such a cool story to tell your friends.

Answer: None of the above! Instead, move as slowly as possible, spread your arms and your legs apart, and float to the top.

Quicksand

TAKE THE QUICKSAND TEST!

1. Quicksand is alive.

   True   false

2. Quicksand will suck you down.

   True   false

3. Once you step in quicksand, you're stuck and can't move.

   True   false

4. Quicksand exists only on Gilligan's Island.

   True   false

5. Quicksand is bottomless.

   True   false

Turn to page 135 for the answers.

Quotes

Great stinkers think alike.

CAN YOU MATCH THESE STINKERS WITH THEIR GREAT THINKERS ON THE FACING PAGE?

(The first one is done for you. Good luck!)

STINKERS

1. I stink, therefore I am. **(answer: f)**

2. The early bird catches the gummy worm.

3. One small step for Astro, one giant leap for Toady.

4. Give me liberty or give me bad breath.

5. I only regret that I have but one giant jawbreaker to lick.

6. May the Smell be with you.

7. Speak softly and carry a big stink.

8. A penny saved is a penny more for Stink.

9. To pee or not to pee, that is the question.

Quotes

GREAT THINKERS

a. "May the Force be with you."
   Obi-Wan Kenobi, *Star Wars*

b. "One small step for man, one giant leap
   for mankind."
   Neil Armstrong

c. "Speak softly and carry a big stick."
   West African proverb made popular by
   Teddy Roosevelt

d. "To be or not to be, that is the question."
   Shakespeare in *Hamlet*

e. "A penny saved is a penny earned."
   Ben Franklin in *Poor Richard's Almanac*

f. "I think, therefore I am."
   René Descartes

g. "Give me liberty or give me death."
   Patrick Henry

h. "The early bird catches the worm."
   Proverb

i. "I only regret that I have but one life
   to lose for my country."
   Nathan Hale

Turn to page 136 for the answers.

R Races

Faster than a speeding . . . car bed?

◎ The Grand Prix is the race to win if you drive a sports car.

◎ The marathon is a 26.2-mile foot race that tests a runner's endurance.

Races

⊚ The Tour de France bicycle race lasts for about three weeks, has about 180 riders making up roughly 20 teams, and covers 3,500 kilometers (2,175 miles)!

⊚ If you've got a sled, a team of dogs, and a good pair of long underwear, you might consider the Iditarod, a 1,150-mile trek across Alaskan wilderness.

⊚ The America's Cup, often called the Oldest Trophy in Sport, is the prize if you like to sail fast boats on high seas.

Races

AND NOW, SOME LESSER-KNOWN RACES:

- ◎ The 10K Mud Run at Camp Pendleton, California, involves racing through an obstacle course, but the biggest challenge of all is slogging through the final 30-foot-long pit, which is filled with knee-high mud!

- ◎ Only cardboard, packing tape, and cleverness can be used to create a kayak that must keep you afloat in the Kardboard Kayak Kup.

HONKK! HONKK!

Races

- In Virginia City, Nevada, you can see not only ostrich racing, but emu racing and camel racing, too.

- Carve a pumpkin, give it some wheels and a push, and watch the good times roll in the annual Rancho Cucamonga, California, Pumpkin Car Race!

- The earliest known turtle race dates from 1924. Turtle racing is still popular, but live turtles have, in many cases, been replaced by the plastic variety. Absolutely no hares are allowed.

Riddles

What has a Stink but doesn't smell? The Moody family, of course! More head-scratching riddles:

1. What can run but never walks, has a mouth but never talks, has a head but never weeps, and has a bed but never sleeps?

2. As I was going to the fair, I met seven jugglers and a bear. Every juggler had six cats, every cat had five rats, every rat had four houses, every house had three mice, every mouse had two louses, every louse had a spouse. How many are going to the fair?

3. There was an airplane crash in which every single person died, but two people survived. How is this possible?

Turn to page 136 for the answers!

Rocks

Stink owns an actual moon rock. If only that rock could talk. The extraterrestrial tales it could tell!

★ The oldest moon rock examined by scientists is said to be 4.5 billion years old. The oldest earth rock is a tot by comparison: 3.8 billion years old.

★ Yogi Rock is not Yogi Bear's best friend. It's a rock on Mars named after the cartoon character because it's shaped like the head of a bear.

★ The most famous rock in *New England* is Plymouth Rock, where the Pilgrims supposedly first set foot.

Rocks

★ The Old Man of the Mountain is a rock formation that looks like the face of an old dude. You can see it on the back of the New Hampshire state quarter. Sadly, the actual Old Man's face fell off in a rock slide in 2003.

★ Uluru (Ayers Rock) is a giant sandstone formation in the middle of Australia. A walk around it covers 5.8 miles. It is sacred to Indigenous Australians.

★ The Hope Diamond is a big fat blue diamond on display in the Smithsonian. It is famous for the curse it puts on the person who wears it. In spite of its bad vibes, this rock is worth 250 million big ones. Ka-ching!

The letter *s* S

If you give a monkey a typewriter . . .

An experiment done in 2003 with six typing monkeys produced five pages of typewriting that were filled mainly with the letter *S*. If you give a monkey enough time, it will likely type out an entire Shakespearean play!

Secret Life of School Supplies

Open up Stink's backpack and who knows what strange and long-lost items might tumble out. A moldy sandwich, an apple core, pieces of eight, a guinea pig? What's in your backpack?

Crayons:

- In the U.S. alone, 12 million crayons are made each day. End to end, those crayons would circle the globe 6 times.

Erasers:

- Before rubber, bread crumbs were used to erase pencil marks!

Glue:

- Standard white school-glue was used to build a bridge made out of pasta that could hold 2,350 pounds.

Pen:

- What writes in a vacuum, without gravity, at extreme temperatures, even upside down, even on Pluto? The Space Pen! It's been used on all manned space flights since its maiden voyage in 1968 on *Apollo VII*.

Secret Life of School Supplies

Pencil:

- One pencil will draw a line that is 35 miles long!

Pencil sharpener:

- African-American inventor John Lee Love invented the portable, hand-held pencil sharpener in 1897.

Highlighter:

- Yukio Horie of Japan invented the highlighter in 1962.

Sticky Notes:

- In 1996, a sticky note found on the nose of an airplane in Minneapolis, made it all the way from Las Vegas. It had survived takeoff and landing, speeds of 500 mph, and -56 degree temperatures.

Ruler:

- Caught without a ruler? No prob! Use a dollar bill. . . . A dollar bill is exactly six inches long. Fold the dollar into thirds, then in half again. Now open it back up and use the creases for one-inch marks.

Shark Bites

Judy: Hey Stink, I once ate shark meat.

Stink: What did the shark do to deserve that?

◎ Great white sharks have about 3,000 teeth. These teeth give them their nickname: Ultimate Assassin.

◎ Sharks chomp down or bite with a force of 6 tons per square inch.

DID YOU KNOW?

For every shark that takes a bite out of a human being, humans kill about a million sharks.

Shark Bites

◎ Sharks can detect one drop of blood in the water from 2.5 miles away!

◎ In 1935, a 14-foot tiger shark in an aquarium in Sydney, Australia, puked up a human arm! How did the police figure out that the arm had belonged to a criminal named James Smith? Simple! There was a tattoo on the arm and fingerprints on the hand.

DID YOU KNOW?

Sharks can go for 6 weeks without taking a bite. One swell shark (in an aquarium) didn't eat for almost a year and a half.

TREASURE HUNT
WINNERS
ANNOUNCED
TODAY

Shipwrecks

Stink and Judy take a ride on Blackbeard's pirate ship. Well, not the real ship. The real wreck of Blackbeard's ship, the *Queen Anne's Revenge,* was discovered at the bottom of the ocean off the coast of North Carolina in 1996.

DID YOU KNOW?

A United Nations report estimates that there are more than 3 million shipwrecks on the ocean floors.

91

Shipwrecks

⚓ It's Friday, May 7, 1915, and you're aboard the mighty "Greyhound of the Seas," sailing from New York to Liverpool, England, when the ship is hit by a German torpedo. The ship, weighing more than 30,000 tons, will sink in a matter of 20 minutes and send close to 1,200 people to their watery graves.

Shipwrecks

⚓ With 90 guns on deck, the "fairest flower of all the ships that ever sailed" sets out on July 19, 1545, as King Henry VIII looks on with pride. You're climbing up to the castle deck when a high wind blows up and capsizes the ship. The gun ports are flooded, and all but 40 of the 500 crew members will lose their lives.

⚓ It's almost midnight on April 14, 1912, and you're standing on deck. The lookout yells, "Iceberg ahead!" Too late. Ice rips into the ship's hull like a can opener. The ship sinks into the depths of the North Atlantic and more than 1,500 people will die.

Turn to page 136 for the answers.

Snot

"Hey, Judy, have you been digitally spelunking in your nasal cavity? It's not polite to pick your nose in public."

"Stink, that's snot even funny!"

"Oh, yes, it is!"

- One finger or two? In the 1500s, books on manners contained tips on the best way to pick your nose!

- Snot is the mucus that lives in your nose. Even kings and queens called it snot, dating back to the 1600s.

Send a booger to a friend!
Through e-mail, that is.
Go to www.pickboogers.com

DID YOU KNOW?

You swallow more than 2 cups of snot per day. And that's on days when you don't even have a cold!

Southpaws

Left-handed people are often thought to be more creative than right-handed people, and more lefties than righties have an IQ higher than 140. Stink is proud to be a lefty!

OTHER FAMOUS LEFTIES:

- ★ Helen Keller
- ★ Michelangelo
- ★ Kermit the Frog
- ★ Barack Obama
- ★ Ben Franklin

- ★ Bart Simpson
- ★ Leonardo da Vinci
- ★ Babe Ruth
- ★ Oprah Winfrey
- ★ Paul McCartney

Eight U.S. presidents were either left-handed or ambidextrous (James Garfield was able to use both hands equally well), and one out of four Apollo astronauts were left-handed.

DID YOU KNOW?

In twins, one is often left-handed.

Southpaws

ARE YOU A SOUTHPAW?

Take the lefty test to find out.

1. Your back itches. Which hand do you use to scratch it?

2. Clap your hands. Which hand is on top?

3. Wink at your friend. Which eye do you wink with?

4. The phone's ringing. Which ear do you listen with?

5. Your hair's a mess. Which hand do you comb it with?

NICKNAMES FOR LEFT-HANDERS IN THE U.K.:

Dolly-pawed

Cuddy-wifter

Spuddy-handed

Cow-pawed

Gibble-fisted

Scrammy-handed

August 13 is International Left-Handers Day.

DID YOU KNOW?

All polar bears are left-handed, making them the truest southpaws!

Space Junk

Here on Earth, the Moody family tries to help clean up the planet by reducing, reusing, and recycling, but who's going to clean up outer space?

★ There's a giant garbage dump orbiting the earth. Four million pounds of stuff from space stations, rockets, and space missions are floating around in the galaxy. Officially, 8,927 objects have been tracked, but by some counts, more than one million pieces of junk are littering space.

★ That extraterrestrial trash is zooming around at speeds of up to 25,000 mph. At that speed, a piece of space junk the size of a tennis ball becomes equal to 25 sticks of dynamite.

Space Junk

★ **Hey! What if a piece of space junk hits me on the head?**

Most space junk that reenters the earth's atmosphere lands over water. Only one person has ever been hit by space junk. In 1997, an Oklahoma woman was hit by a piece of metal from the fuel tank of a Delta II rocket.

URP!

Sports

Stink likes to be different, which is why he prefers karate to baseball, soccer, or basketball. If you're looking to sweat with style, here are some other great choices:

- You may have enjoyed a game of thumb-wrestling from time to time, but did you know that you can go pro through the World Finger Jousting Federation?

Sports

◎ The Mobile Phone Throwing World Championship takes place in Savonlinna, Finland, every August. One distance event winner hurled a cell phone 294 feet.

◎ Feeling spudly? If you like the feeling of mashed potatoes in your hair and your nostrils and your shorts, then Mashed Potato Wrestling is the sport for you.

◎ If your strength is in your elbows, not your thumbs, then you might do better at Elbow Racing. Crouch down on your knees, place your elbows on the ground, put your hands over your ears, and GO!

T Treasure Hunts

Ahoy, mateys! Want to find buried treasure without having to stow away on the Moody family vacation to Ocracoke Island? Treasure hunters unite!

You'll love the new sport of geocaching, a high-tech treasure hunt. This exciting outdoor sport started in the year 2000, and there are now hundreds of thousands of active caches worldwide.

Treasure Hunts

GEO is for geography. **CACHING** is for hiding a cache (a bunch) of stuff. All you need are a sense of adventure and a GPS system. If you don't have a GPS system, you can join a local hunt that will provide you with one for the day.

Take along a map, a compass, a pen, and a grown-up to help you.

To get started, go to www.geocaching.com and type in your zip code to find a cache near you. This site lists over 250,000 caches all over the world!

Treasure Hunts

Bring a small item to add to the cache when you find it. A few ideas:

- Baseball card
- Fridge magnet
- Key chain
- Matchbox car
- Action figure
- Foreign coin
- Mini flashlight
- Wind-up robot
- Polished rock or gem
- Trading card
- Eraser
- Yo-yo
- Pirate ring
- Dollar bill
- Marble
- Deck of cards
- Mini-book

Treasure Hunts

Don't forget to sign the logbook
to show that you found the cache.

Note: Many caches include a
throw-away camera. If you find
one, go ahead and take your
picture. That will be proof that
you really found the cache!

DID YOU KNOW?

A geomuggle
is someone
who
stumbles on
a geocache.
Some caches
are stolen
or moved by
geomuggles!
This is a
no-no.

Tsunamis

Stink is big on weather. He's even bigger on *big* weather. These storms will blow you away!

A tsunami is a gigantic wave or a wall of water triggered by an earthquake, a landslide, an explosion, or a volcanic eruption. In Alaska on July 9, 1958, an earthquake triggered a landslide which created a tsunami wave that was 1,720 feet tall, taller than any skyscraper on Earth at that time.

One of these mega-waves can travel 500 mph, faster than a jet airplane. In 1960, tsunami waves traveled from Chile to Japan, covering 10,500 miles in less than a day.

Tsunamis can also be caused by asteroid impact. The asteroid that created the Chicxulub Crater in Yucatan about 65 million years ago may have triggered the largest mega-tsunami ever.

DID YOU KNOW?

60% of all tsunamis take place in the Pacific Ocean.

Tsunamis

The deadliest tsunami took place on December 26, 2004. It was triggered by an earthquake in the Indian Ocean and killed 283,100 people.

The now-famous story of Owen and Mzee took place during that same tsunami. A young hippo named Owen got separated from his family. When taken to Haller Park in Kenya, he struck up a friendship with Mzee, a 130-year-old tortoise. They swim, eat, and play together, and have their own unique way of communicating.

U Underdogs

Stink, aka Captain Pluto of Pluto and the Underdogs, knows how great it must have felt when these underdogs all came out on top!

"Miracle on Ice!"

During the 1980 Olympics, a team of young, amateur ice hockey players from the United States did the impossible: they beat the best hockey team in the world, the Soviet Union.

President Thomas E. Dewey!

That's what *Life* magazine and the *New York Times* declared before the final results of the 1948 U.S. presidential election were in. Oops! Once the votes were counted, the winner was Harry S. Truman.

He's Back!

Back in the early 1700s, hundreds of thousands of bald eagles thrived in the United States wilderness. By 1963, there were barely 400 nesting pairs of bald eagles left. Today, the United States is again home to some 10,000 nesting pairs.

Underdogs

The Incredible Journey
At age 18, Canadian Terry Fox lost a leg to cancer. Three years later, with the help of an artificial leg, Terry began his "Marathon of Hope": a run across Canada to raise money for cancer research. He ran an average of 23.3 miles per day every day for 143 days, and raised 24 million dollars.

Aiming High
Climbing the world's highest mountains is not only difficult, but dangerous. So imagine being Erik Weihenmayer, who's scaled them successfully without being able to see. Erik has been blind since age 13.

Undies

Stink wears them. Judy wears them. You wear them. (You do, don't you?) Even Astro the guinea pig once wore a pair of underwear!

If the word UNDERWEAR makes you blush, don't get your Grundies in a bunch. Try these words on for size instead!

- unmentionables
- Skivvies
- briefs
- snuggles
- wedgie riders
- gitch
- gruds
- knickers
- Grundies
- Reg Grundies

- drawers
- scanties
- tighty whities
- smalls
- speedo
- gotch
- bloomers
- trolleys
- Reginalds

DID YOU KNOW?

Up until a few years ago, crash dummies in the U.S. had to wear pink undies.

110

Undies

WHAT'S UNDER ALL THAT ARMOR?

In medieval times, knights wore baggy undershorts called braies.

BONE APPÉTIT?

Undies are right up there on the top ten list of things dogs like to chew on.

- socks
- panty hose
- balls
- corncobs
- hair ties / ribbons
- underwear
- rocks
- chew toys
- bones
- sticks

V Virginia Roadside Attractions

Stink ♥ Virginia. Let him count the ways.

VIRGINIA HAS GIANTS!

ATTRACTION	HEIGHT	LOCATION
giant coffee pot	15 feet	Roanoke
giant watering can	20 feet	Alexandria
giant Johnny Appleseed	10 feet	New Market
giant apple on a stick	24 feet	Thaxton
giant roller skate	9 feet	Morrisville
giant pencil	30 feet	Wytheville
giant sea serpent	40 feet	Sandbridge
giant clothespin	10 feet	Richmond

IS MOUNT TRASHMORE

a. a park?
b. a trash dump?
c. a mountain?

Turn to page 136 for the answer!

Virginia Roadside Attractions

VERY NICE VENUES TO VISIT WHILE VACATIONING IN VIRGINIA:

FOAMHENGE. You mean Stonehenge? No, Foamhenge. In the town of Natural Bridge, you can get your picture taken next to this crazy replica of Stonehenge made out of 16-foot blocks of foam.

STYROTOWN. You mean Storytown? No, Styrotown. Colonial Beach was once home to an entire miniature town made from Styrofoam, toothpicks, and acrylic paint, lit by hundreds of lights at night.

DR PEPPER, R.I.P. In Rural Retreat, you can visit the grave of the pharmacist Dr. Charles Taylor Pepper, who was the inspiration for the famous soda drink.

WAVE GOOD-BYE

STONEWALL JACKSON'S ARM. Yep, just his arm. It has its own grave in Chancellorsville.

Volcanoes

Whenever Stink gets mad—really, really mad!—he blows his top. (On the VEI scale, I'd say that tantrum was an 8.)

★ One way to measure volcanic eruptions is the VEI. VEI stands for Volcanic Explosivity Index. It's a scale from 0-8; the higher the number, the larger the explosion.

★ In 1883, Krakatoa, in Indonesia, exploded with a force about 13,000 times as powerful as an atomic bomb. The explosion was so loud that it was heard in Australia, over 5,000 kilometers (3,107 miles) away.

★ The most active volcanic area in the world is called the Ring of Fire, which is located around the edge of the Pacific Plate.

DID YOU KNOW?

There are volcanoes on other planets! The largest known volcano in the solar system, Olympus Mons, is on Mars, and is 16 miles high.

Volcanoes

Hawaii was formed by undersea volcanoes and contains both the world's largest dormant volcano and the world's most active volcano.

DID YOU KNOW?

Someone who studies volcanoes is called a volcanologist.

W Weather

> Judy: Hey, shrinky Stink, how's the weather down there?
>
> Stink: Just fine, thanks!

Hottest Year on Record

2005

Coldest Temperature Ever Recorded

July 21, 1983: Vostok Station in Antarctica
–128.6 degrees F (–89.2 C)

Worst Hail Storm

July, 1984: Munich, Germany
Hail the size of baseballs fell from the sky, causing 1 billion dollars worth of damage.

Weather

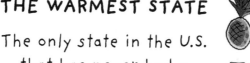

THE WARMEST STATE

The only state in the U.S. that has never had a temperature drop below zero is Hawaii.

The Most Cows Killed by Lightning

On Halloween day in 2005, sixty-eight cows in New South Wales, Australia, were killed when a nearby tree was struck by lightning.

Baseball-shaped Lightning

The ancient Greeks saw strange glowing balls streak across the sky. Others throughout history have reported seeing these, too. What they saw is called ball (or globe) lightning, usually about the size of a baseball.

Word Games

Stink's smelly sneakers stunk like a skunk's. Trip up your tongue with tons of tricky tongue-twisters:

Judy Moody's cooties.

Toady tidied up after toasting tangleberry tarts.

Astro asked for aspirin after eating ants.

Mouse was mainly moody but not as mega-moody as Judy.

Jaws just juiced a giant jawbreaker.

Slimy, slippery salamanders slithered down the stinky sewer.

A skunk sat on a stump and thunk the stump stunk, but the stump thunk the skunk stunk.

The sixth sick sheik's sixth sheep's sick. (This is said to be the most difficult tongue-twister in the English language.)

DID YOU KNOW?

TYPEWRITER can be typed using just the top row of letters on a keyboard. So can PEPPERROOT and TEETER-TOTTER.

Word Games

Stink's mom and dad are a couple of palindromes! Palindromes are words, phrases, or sentences that say the same thing spelled backward or forward:

★ Go hang a salami, I'm a lasagna hog.

★ poop

★ Step on no pets.

★ May a moody baby doom a yam.

★ eye

★ Rats live on no evil star.

★ toot

★ Was it Eliot's toilet I saw?

★ race car

★ straw warts

★ Debate with girls last; if it's all right, I wet a bed.

DID YOU KNOW?

Quartzy is the highest-scoring word in Scrabble.

X X-treme Sports!

Stink is X-tremely sure he's going to stick with karate, thank you very much!

◎ It took eleven tries, but Tony Hawk is the first person ever to complete a 900-degree turn on a skateboard. That's two-and-a-half full turns in the air!

◎ Robbie Knievel succeeded in jumping the fountain at Caesars Palace in Las Vegas on a motorcycle, a jump that once landed his father, Evel Knievel, in a coma for twenty-nine days.

◎ When Kit DesLauriers skied down Mt. Everest, she became the first person to ever have skied down the Seven Summits: the highest peak on each of the seven continents.

X-treme Sports!

THE LARGEST NUMBER OF SKYDIVES MADE
BY ONE PERSON IN ONE DAY IS:

    a. 6   b. 46

    c. 64   d. 640

Turn to page 136 for the answer.

Y Youngest

Stink is the youngest member of his family, and Judy never lets him forget it!

If you're the youngest kid in the family, you are said to be:

- a risk-taker
- not one to give up
- fond of attention
- creative
- a great storyteller
- competitive
- outgoing, social
- spoiled, babied
- easily bored
- funny

YOUNGEST PERSON TO BECOME A DOCTOR

Balamurali Ambati graduated from NYU at age 13 and medical school at 17, becoming the youngest doctor in the world in 1995.

YOUNGEST PERSON TO SAIL SOLO ACROSS THE ATLANTIC OCEAN

Michael Perham, from England, crossed the 3,500 miles of Atlantic Ocean in his yacht, the *Cheeky Monkey,* in 2007 at age 14.

Youngest

YOUNGEST BILLIONAIRE

Prince Albert von Thurn und Taxis turned 18 in 2001 and inherited a fortune. According to a 2007 *Forbes* magazine, he's worth 2 billion dollars.

YOUNGEST PERSON TO CLIMB MOUNT EVEREST

Temba Tsheri of Nepal reached the summit of Mount Everest in 2001 at age 16.

DID YOU KNOW?

Peter Reynolds is fourteen minutes younger than his twin brother, Paul.

Z ZAP!

Hair-raising hair frizzer!

Stink's spiked hair kind of makes it look like he's been hit by lightning. What's his secret? Gobs of hair gel.

NO HAIR GEL CAN FIX THIS

★ Roy Sullivan has survived seven lightning strikes. His hair has even caught on fire!

★ Every minute, 1,800 thunderstorms are taking place on Earth. Each storm gives off an average of 100 lightning bolts.

★ Look out, King Kong! Lightning strikes the Empire State Building about 100 times a year.

★ Roughly 73 people are killed and 300 are injured by lightning each year in the United States.

ZAP!

THE EIGHT TYPES OF LIGHTNING:

- forked
- streak
- ball
- sheet
- heat
- chain
- crawler
- ribbon

BE PREPARED!

Do you know what to do in a lightning storm? Test your readiness:

1. Don't stand near a tree.
   True   False

2. Stay in the car.
   True   False

3. Hold up an umbrella.
   True   False

4. Go sailing.
   True   False

5. Wear rubber boots.
   True   False

6. Fly a kite and discover electricity.
   True   False

7. Don't take a shower.
   True   False

8. Dress up as the Tin Man.
   True   False

9. Stand in a puddle.
   True   False

10. Don't talk on the phone.
    True   False

Turn to page 137 for the answer.

Zombie Jokes

Stink: Knock-knock!
Judy: Who's there?
Stink: Zombie.
Judy: Zombie who?
Stink: Zom-bee is buzzing around your head! Hope he doesn't sting you!
Judy: Hardee-har-har.

Do zombies eat popcorn with their fingers?
No, they eat the fingers separately.

What kind of street do most zombies live on?
Dead ends.

How do zombies predict the future?
They read their horrorscope in the paper.

What do zombies like to eat at a cookout?
Halloweenies.

What was the zombie doing at the post office?
He heard they have a lot of dead letters.

What did the baby zombie call her parents?
Mummy and Deady.

Zombie Jokes

What happens when a zombie catches a cold?
He buys coffin drops.

What did the zombie have in his rock collection?
Gravestones.

Where do zombies like to swim?
Lake Eerie.

What did the zombie give his mother for Mother's Day?
A bouquet of corpse flowers.

Wondering which books inspired the entries in *Stink-O-Pedia: Volume 2*? Take a look! How many of them have *you* read?

Stink: The Incredible Shrinking Kid

Big and Little
LOL
Monsters
Newts and Other State
    Amphibians
Underdogs
Youngest

Stink and the Incredible Super Galactic Jawbreaker

Earwax
Glow in the Dark
Ka-Ching!
Quotes

Stink and the World's Worst Super-Stinky Sneakers

Dirty, Stinky, Yucky Jobs
Invisible Ink
Pop Poop Quiz
Snot

Stink and the Great Guinea Pig Express

Great Wall of China
Secret Life of School Supplies
Undies
Virginia Roadside Attractions

Judy Moody & Stink: The Holly Joliday

Freaks of Nature
Homework Excuses
Jack Frost
Night Owls
Pizza
Tsunamis
Weather
ZAP!

Judy Moody & Stink: The Mad, Mad, Mad, Mad Treasure Hunt

Lighthouses
Quicksand
Races
Riddles
Shipwrecks
Treasure Hunts
Word Games

Stink-O-Pedia, Volume 1

Leap Year
Zombie Jokes

These things all come from books starring Stink's moody big sister, Judy. See if you can figure out which titles they come from!

Brainy Cat

Carnivorous Plants

Cars

Disasters

Hairy Facts

Insects

Knuckleheads

Nerds of the World, Unite!

Origami

Rocks

The Letter S

Shark Bites

Volcanoes

And look for these other Stink-y topics in new and forthcoming books about Stink and Judy Moody:

Animals in Space

Fingerprinting

Mnemonics

Outer Space Jokes

Southpaws

Space Junk

Sports

X-treme Sports

Selected Sources

Books:

Aronson, Marc, and HP Newquist. *For Boys Only: The Biggest, Baddest Book Ever.* New York: Feiwel and Friends, 2007.

The Bathroom Readers' Institute. *Uncle John's Strange and Scary Bathroom Reader for Kids Only!* Ashland, OR: Bathroom Readers' Press, 2006.

Becker, Helaine. *Boredom Blasters: Brain Bogglers, Awesome Activities, Cool Comics, Tasty Treats, and More . . .* Illustrated by Claudia Davila. Toronto: Maple Tree Press, 2004.

Buckley, James, and Robert Stremme. *Scholastic Book of Lists, New and Updated.* New York: Scholastic Reference, 2006.

Carson, Mary Kay. *Extreme Planets Q&A.* Smithsonian Q&A series. New York, Collins, 2008

Glenday, Craig, ed. *Guinness World Records 2007.* New York: Bantam Books, 2007.

Ho, Oliver. *Mutants and Monsters.* Mysteries Unwrapped series. Illustrated by Josh Cochran. New York: Sterling, 2008.

Horne, Richard, and Tracey Turner. *101 Things You Need to Know . . . and Some You Don't!* New York: Walker Books for Young Readers, 2007.

House, Katherine L. *Lighthouses for Kids.* Chicago: Chicago Review Press, 2008

Janeczko, Paul B. *Top Secret: A Handbook of Codes, Ciphers, and Secret Writing.* Illustrated by Jenna LaReau. Cambridge, MA: Candlewick Press, 2004.

Joyce, C. Alan, ed. *The World Almanac for Kids 2008.* Mahwah, NJ: World Almanac Books, 2008.

Lambert, David, and the Diagram Group. *Super Little Giant Book of Secret Codes.* New York: Sterling, 2007.

MacDonald, Guy. *Even More Children's Miscellany.* Illustrated by Niki Catlow. San Francisco: Chronicle Books, 2008.

Masoff, Joy. *Oh, Yikes! History's Grossest, Wackiest Moments.* Illustrated by Terry Sirrell. New York: Workman Publishing, 2006.

Selected Sources

————. *Oh, Yuck! The Encyclopedia of Everything Nasty.* Illustrated by Terry Sirrell. New York: Workman Publishing, 2000.

McCutcheon, Marc. *The Kid Who Named Pluto: And the Stories of Other Extraordinary Young People in Science.* Illustrated by Jon Cannell. San Francisco: Chronicle Books, 2008.

Mooney, Julie, and the editors of Ripley's Believe It or Not! *The World of Ripley's Believe It or Not!* New York: Black Dog and Leventhal, 1999.

Morgan, Matthew, and Samantha Barnes. *Children's Miscellany Too: More Useless Information That's Essential to Know.* Illustrated by Niki Catlow. San Francisco: Chronicle Books, 2006.

Nguyen, Duy, and Tramy Nguyen. *Junk Mail Origami.* New York: Sterling, 2008.

Ramos-Elorduy, Julieta. *Creepy Crawly Cuisine: The Gourmet Guide to Edible Insects.* Rochester, VT: Park Street Press, 1998.

Rifkin, Josh. *Xtreme Sports: A Quiz Deck.* Beverly Hills, CA: Pomegranate, 2007.

Rowen, Beth. *Time for Kids Almanac 2008.* New York: Time for Kids Books, 2008.

Scott, Elaine. *When Is a Planet not a Planet? The Story of Pluto.* New York: Clarion Books, 2007.

Stillman, Janice, ed. *The Old Farmer's Almanac for Kids.* Dublin, NH: Yankee Publishing, 2005.

Temko, Florence. *Kirigami.* New York: Platt & Munk, 1962.

Townsend, John. *Foolish Physics: A Weird History of Science.* Chicago: Raintree, 2006.

————. *Outrageous Inventions: A Weird History of Science.* Chicago: Raintree, 2006.

Whitehead, Sarah. *How to Speak Cat.* New York: Scholastic, 2008.

Selected Sources

Websites:

http://50states.com *(accessed January 19, 2010).*

Discovery Channel. http://dsc.discovery.com/ *(accessed January 19, 2010).*

Enchanted Learning. http://www.enchantedlearning.com/home.html *(accessed January 19, 2010).*

Guinness World Records. http://www.guinnessworldrecords.com *(accessed January 19, 2010).*

How Stuff Works. http://www.howstuffworks.com/ *(accessed January 19, 2010).*

Leap Year Day. http://leapyearday.com *(accessed January 19, 2010).*

National Geograpic Kids. http://kids.nationalgeographic.com/ *(accessed January 19, 2010).*

Nova Online. http://www.pbs.org/wgbh/nova/ *(accessed January 19, 2010).*

PBS Kids. http://pbskids.org/ *(accessed January 19, 2010).*

http://space.com/ *(accessed January 19, 2010).*

Answers

p. 8: Is Your Cat a Genius?
Yes. A scent map, that is. Cats can find their way home from hundreds of miles away by following scents.

Yes. A cat is smart enough to learn where the food comes from.

Yes. Cats nap 13–18 hours a day, and taking naps makes you smarter.

Yes. If your cat does not like something—getting sprayed for fleas or taking a pill—good luck trying it a second time. Your cat will remember!

Yes. Who needs a clock when your cat can wake you at the same time every day?

Yes. So your cat has YOU trained. How smart is that?

Yes. And that's a sign of emotional intelligence. Your cat can communicate anxiety, fear, curiosity, and anger with its ears.

p. 33: The Buzz on Mosquitoes
a. a kid
b. a blond person
b. someone wearing a black shirt
a. someone who just ate a banana
b. someone who just ran a marathon
Foods high in potassium—like bananas—and exercising cause your body to release lactic acid, which is attractive to mosquitoes.

p. 35: Can you read the message below?
(Of course not—it's invisible!)

Answers

p. 42: Knuckleheads

1. White
2. George Washington
3. I-T
4. Peacocks don't lay eggs; peahens do.
5. *Incorrectly*
6. Yes, every year right after the third of July.
7. He had the same name then as he does now.
8. None. Noah had the ark.
9. Corn
10. Underground
11. When it's an elephant
12. Wet
13. Edam (a type of cheese) is the word *made* spelled backward.

p. 72: Pop Poop Quiz

1. b. pigeon poop
2. c. water
3. a. a car
4. b. They have to eat twice to get all their vitamins.
5. a. gunpowder
6. a. guinea pig
7. c. They froze it into poop-sicles.
8. All of the above
9. a. President Harry S. Truman.

p. 74: The Quicksand Test

All are false. Each is a common myth about quicksand.

Answers

p. 77: Quotes
1. f
2. h
3. b
4. g
5. i
6. a
7. c
8. e
9. d

p. 82: Riddles
1. A river.
2. Only one is going to the fair: the narrator.
3. Two of the passengers were married, not single.

pp. 92–93: What's the name of your ship?
The *Lusitania;* the *Mary Rose;* the *Titanic*

p. 112: Mount Trashmore
All of the above! Virginia Beach turned an ugly, smelly 125-acre, 60-foot high landfill into a beautiful city park named Mount Trashmore.

p. 121: Skydiving
The largest number of skydives made by one person in one day is **d. 640!**

Answers

p. 125: Test Your Lightning Readiness

1. True
2. True
3. False (Metal conducts electricity.)
4. False (Keep away from open water.)
5. True (Rubber does not conduct electricity.)
6. False (Do not stay out in the open.)
7. True (Water conducts electricity.)
8. False (What did we say about metal?)
9. False (What did we say about water?)
10. True (Lightning seeks electrical and metallic places to discharge.)

Be sure to check out Stink's adventures!

He has his own series and his own website.

www.stinkmoody.com

Need more Moody? Try these!

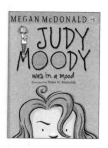

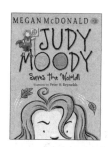
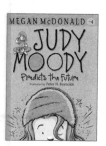

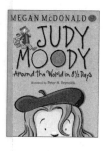

First edition 2010

Library of Congress Cataloging-in-Publication Data is available.
Library of Congress Catalog Card Number pending
ISBN 978-0-7636-4558-8

10 11 12 13 14 15 RRC 10 9 8 7 6 5 4 3 2 1
Printed in Crawfordsville, IN, U.S.A.

This book was typeset in Stone Informal and Providence Sans.
The illustrations were created digitally.

Candlewick Press
99 Dover Street
Somerville, Massachusetts 02144

visit us at www.candlewick.com